Life of the Ladybug

Life of the Ladybug

by Heiderose and Andreas Fischer-Nagel

A Carolrhoda Nature Watch Book

Carolrhoda Books, Inc./Minneapolis

Thanks to Jerry Heaps, Registered Professional Entomologist,
for his assistance with this book

This edition first published 1986 by Carolrhoda Books, Inc.
Original edition published 1981 by Kinderbuchverlag KBV Luzern AG,
Lucerne, Switzerland, under the title MARIENKÄFER DIE
WUNDERBARE VERWANDLUNG AUS DEM EI © 1981
Translation from the German © 1981 by J. M. Dent & Sons Ltd.
Adapted by Carolrhoda Books, Inc.
All rights reserved

LIBRARY OF CONGRESS CATALOGING IN PUBLICATION DATA

Fischer-Nagel, Heiderose.
  Life of the ladybug.

  Includes glossary.
  Translation of: Marienkäfer.
  "A Carolrhoda nature watch book."
  Summary: An introduction to the physical character-
istics and life cycle of the ladybug.
  1. Ladybirds—Juvenile literature. [1. Ladybugs]
I. Fischer-Nagel, Andreas. II. Title.
QL596.C65F5713 1986   595.76'9   85-25467
  ISBN 0-87614-240-4

1 2 3 4 5 6 7 8 9 10 94 93 92 91 90 89 88 87 86

For Tamarica

Life of the Ladybug

In most gardens that have a variety of plants, there are also many different kinds of animals. Some of them, like birds, are easy to see. Others, such as spiders and insects, are harder to find. Although insects are no less common than birds, most of them are so small that they are easily overlooked. In fact, insects are the most numerous of all the world's animals, and every garden contains large numbers of them.

This book is about one particular group of insects—ladybugs. Most kinds of ladybugs are shiny red and black, but there are others with different colors, such as black and yellow or pale brown and yellow.

Like all insects, ladybugs are seen most often in summer, but they begin to get active in spring, as soon as the weather starts to warm up. One day there are no ladybugs anywhere, and the next day, you may see dozens wandering over a flower or clustered together on a fence or a wall.

Throughout the winter, ladybugs are in an inactive state called **hibernation**. Like most insects, ladybugs do not like cold weather, so as soon as winter arrives, they seek shelter. They might hibernate under the loose bark of an old tree, or in the corner of a shed, or sometimes even in a house.

Hundreds of ladybugs often hibernate together, side by side. By lowering their body temperatures and becoming inactive, they can conserve enough energy to survive the cold weather. It's best not to disturb hibernating ladybugs because, as you'll see later, they are among the most useful and attractive of all the insects.

With the arrival of spring and warmer weather, the ladybugs awaken from hibernation and become active again. Everywhere in gardens and parks, these colorful insects can be seen on flowers, bushes, and in the grass as they resume their active lives.

Besides hunting for food, one of the first things ladybugs do after they emerge from hibernation is to seek out their mates. This way, a new generation of ladybugs can be born within a short time.

The photograph above shows a group of common seven-spot ladybugs. Because their colors are the same, male and female ladybugs are not easy to tell apart, although the female is sometimes slightly larger than the male. The ladybug in the middle of the picture is probably a female.

Like most insects, ladybugs have poor eyesight, except close up. They probably find and recognize one another mainly by scent and touch. They do this with the help of their short **antennae**, or feelers, which you can see on the head of the ladybug on the left. When the male and female meet, they may sit facing each other for some time.

After a while, the male crawls around behind the female and climbs onto her back. He holds himself in position with his legs, which end in tiny claws. Then he injects a liquid containing **sperm** into the female's body. The sperm, or male reproductive cells, **fertilize** the **egg cells**, or female reproductive cells. The female has had the eggs inside her all the time, but they need the sperm to make them fertile and capable of producing young ladybugs.

Soon after mating, the female ladybug seeks out several places to lay her eggs, usually on plant leaves or stems. Each egg has a sticky substance on it that holds it in position. Females produce several hundred eggs and lay them in different places in small batches ranging from two or three to several dozen. In this way, the female increases their chances of survival since some small animals eat ladybug eggs. If the female laid all her eggs in the same place, it is possible that they would all be eaten at one time. By spreading them out, it is more likely that some will go undetected and survive.

Like most insects, ladybugs go through a complicated process of development called **metamorphosis**, which begins with an egg. From this egg, a ladybug **larva** will hatch and go through the second stage of development. It is during the larval stage that a ladybug does all of its growing. As it grows, the larva sheds its outer covering, called an **exoskeleton**, which does not grow. When it sheds the exoskeleton for the fourth time, a **pupa** is revealed, and the ladybug begins the third stage of metamorphosis. It is during this stage that, beneath a protective shell, the larva changes into an adult ladybug. When this transformation has been completed, in about five days, an adult ladybug emerges from the pupal shell. The fourth and final stage of metamorphosis is the adult ladybug.

Although ladybug eggs are bright yellow at first, they soon turn white as the time comes for them to hatch. The eggs hatch after about a week. The ladybug larvae struggle out of their shells and then rest for a while, until their skin has hardened and darkened.

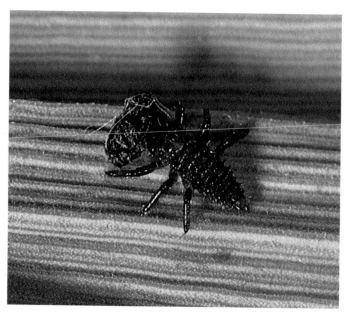

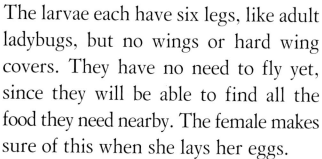

The larvae each have six legs, like adult ladybugs, but no wings or hard wing covers. They have no need to fly yet, since they will be able to find all the food they need nearby. The female makes sure of this when she lays her eggs.

After an hour or so, the ladybug larvae leave their empty eggshells and start to explore their surroundings. Ladybug larvae are fussy about their food. They eat only **aphids** (small, soft-bodied insects) and other plant-eating bugs.

The ladybug larva has plenty of food to choose from, since aphids are all around it. At first, though, when the larva is very small, it chooses the smaller, more tender greenfly aphid as food. It feeds on them by piercing each body with its hollow **mandibles**, or biting jaws, and sucking out its juices. Aphids can be great pests in the garden, and ladybugs help reduce their numbers.

Ladybugs aren't the only insects that like aphids—so do ants, but for a different reason. Ants eat the sweet liquid, called **honeydew**, that the aphids get rid of while they are feeding on plants. Aphids take in more nourishment than they actually need and excrete a liquid that is rich in sugars.

Ants are naturally jealous of anything that threatens their food source. If a ladybug larva attacks a colony of aphids, the ants may try to drive it away or kill it by biting it with their sharp jaws. Ladybug larvae taste so unpleasant, though, that it is unlikely many will actually be killed by the ants. The larvae's bristly hairs may also protect them to some extent.

(1)

(4)

(2)

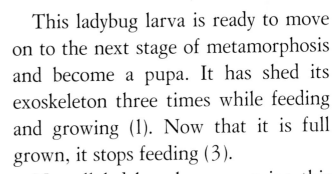

(3)

This ladybug larva is ready to move on to the next stage of metamorphosis and become a pupa. It has shed its exoskeleton three times while feeding and growing (1). Now that it is full grown, it stops feeding (3).

Not all ladybug larvae survive this far. Some are killed and eaten by animals like the fierce lacewing larva (2). If it escapes such dangers, the full-grown ladybug larva now attaches itself to a plant or twig by means of a silky pad (4). There it sits very still until the larval skin splits open to reveal the pupa beneath (5).

Already the outline of the future adult ladybug's head and wing covers

can be seen on the surface of the pupa. Inside the pupa, complicated changes are taking place. The whole structure of the larva is being broken down and rearranged to form the adult ladybug. Then, after about five days, comes the final dramatic change. The pupal shell splits open between the lobes of the head, and the adult beetle pushes its way out, thrusting aside the pupal shell with its legs (6 and 7).

At first the ladybug is yellow or pale orange, but coloring matter will gradually be pumped into the outer skin to change it to its final colors. The skin is soft at first, but it gradually hardens (8).

Here you can see a ladybug that has just freed itself from its pupal shell. Because it is yellow, you might not think it *was* a ladybug at this stage, except for its typical ladybug shape.

The ladybug's spots gradually become clearer. It stretches its wings to allow them to dry and harden properly because it is unable to fly while they are damp.

The curved wing covers protect the delicate wings from damage, covering them when they are not being used. When the ladybug flies, its wing covers are held up high, out of the way of the wings.

29

After several hours, the ladybug has become its final color. The middle section of its body, the **thorax** (the area just behind its head), its wing cases, and its undersides are hard and shiny.

The colors of individual **species**, or kinds, of ladybugs tend to vary. Some are orange-red, while others are a darker red. Still others are black or brown. These ladybugs are all of the seven-spot variety.

Here an adult ladybug is eating a meal of aphids. Adult ladybugs eat large numbers of these harmful insects by chewing them up whole. They do not eat quite as many as their larvae eat, though, because larvae need more food for growth and development. Adult ladybugs have finished growing and need nourishment only for walking, flying, and mating. As you can see, both larvae and adult ladybugs are extremely important pest controllers.

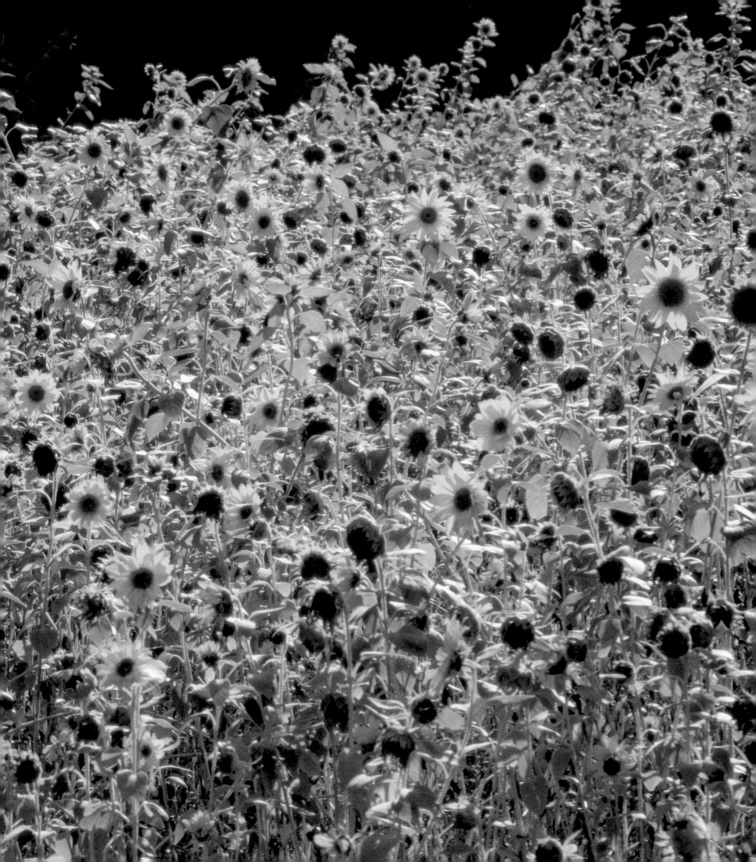

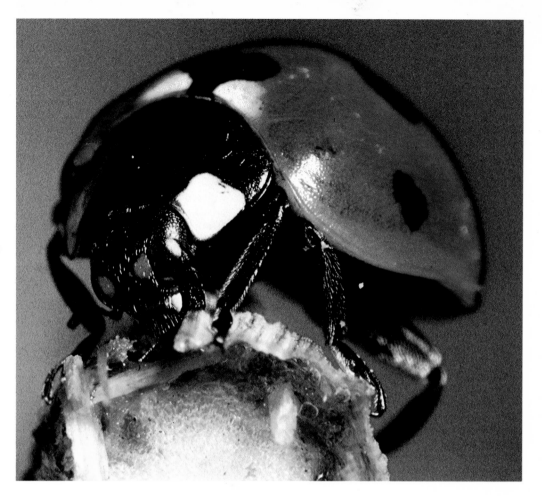

There are not always enough ladybugs to kill all of the aphids that attack plants. Because of this, gardeners and farmers often use **insecticides**. Unfortunately, such poisons are likely to kill ladybugs too, as well as other useful creatures such as spiders and birds.

One of the best ways to control or reduce pests is to increase the numbers of their natural enemies. Since ladybugs eat such large numbers of pests, they and other useful insects have been bred in great numbers and then released onto plants. They have actually been used as natural pest controllers in many countries. They have proved useful in the United States, Australia, and South Africa for controlling **scale insects**, which are plant-eating pests.

This picture shows the difference in size between a ladybug and a small tortoiseshell butterfly. The butterfly is feeding on the sunflower's nectar, and it is likely that the ladybugs are searching for food, too.

All of the ladybugs in this picture are of the seven-spot variety. However, there are many other kinds of ladybugs—about 4,000 species occur in different parts of the world. In the United States there are about 150 kinds; in Europe about 80.

Ladybugs are sometimes referred to by the number of spots they have on their wing covers. The ladybug above is the fourteen-spot. The ladybug below is the much more common two-spot. You can often see this kind in large numbers, especially when they hibernate during the winter.

The large ladybug opposite is sometimes called the "eyed ladybug" because of the eyelike markings on its wing covers. Found mainly on fir trees, it is the largest European ladybug, being about 1/3 to 1/2 inch (8 to 12 mm) long.

The handsomely patterned ladybug opposite is another kind of fourteen-spot, although its spots run together.

Here (top) is one form of the ten-spot ladybug. It is more often yellow with black spots.

The ladybug on the right (middle) has four spots, two on each wing cover.

This black and yellow ladybug (bottom) has 25 spots. It has 9 spots on each wing cover, another where its wing covers join at the top, and 6 more on its thorax. It is less round than most ladybugs and is found in marshy areas.

This seven-spot ladybug looks as if it is dead, but it is only pretending. Ladybugs often do this when danger is near. They fall to the ground, lie still for a moment on their backs, and then turn over and walk or fly away.

Adult ladybugs have other defenses, too. They can give out a horrible-tasting fluid from joints in their bodies that keeps their enemies from eating them. It is thought that the ladybug's bright colors warn birds and other **predators** that it tastes unpleasant and is best avoided.

Most ladybugs born during the summer live for only three or four weeks. When the colder weather comes, those adults that survive go into hibernation for the winter and live longer—about six months.

For centuries, people have believed that ladybugs bring good luck. Perhaps this is because one of the most common species of ladybugs is the seven-spot, and seven has always been considered a lucky number.

The next time you're outside during the summer, you'll probably be able to spot many ladybugs as they go about their work eating plant pests.

Glossary

antennae: jointed, moveable sense organs on the heads of insects

aphids: small, soft-bodied insects that feed on the juice of plants

egg cells: female reproductive cells

exoskeleton: the supportive, protective outer framework of an insect's body

hibernate: to pass the winter in an inactive state. During hibernation, all body functions slow down.

honeydew: a sweet substance that is excreted by aphids. It is a by-product of their digestive process.

insecticide: any substance that is used to kill insects

larva: the second stage of metamorphosis. During this stage, the insect is wormlike and has no wings. The plural form of this word is larvae.

mandibles: the biting jaws of an insect

metamorphosis: the four-stage process of development undergone by many insects. The four stages are: (1) egg, (2) larva, (3) pupa, and (4) adult.

predator: an animal that kills other animals for its food

pupa: the third stage of metamorphosis. During this stage, the larva changes into an adult insect.

scale insects: any of a large group of insects that feed on plants

species: a group of plants or animals that share similar characteristics

sperm: male reproductive cells

thorax: the middle section of an insect's body located between the head and the abdomen

About the Authors

Heiderose and Andreas Fischer-Nagel received degrees in biology from the University of Berlin. Their special interests include animal behavior, wildlife protection, and environmental control. The Fischer-Nagels have collaborated on several internationally successful science books for children. They attribute the success of their books to their "love of children and of our threatened environment" and believe that "children learning to respect nature today are tomorrow's protectors of nature."

The Fischer-Nagels live in Germany with their daughters, Tamarica and Cosmea Désirée.